Semblance

A play

John H. Newmeir

Samuel French—London
New York-Toronto-Hollywood

ISBN 0 573 03385 4

Please see page iv for further copyright information

SEMBLANCE OF MADNESS!

First performed by Adelphi Players at the Focus
Theatre, Southend-on-Sea on 2nd March, 1998, with
the following cast:

Jones	Gwen Wilkes
Hannah	Ann Newmeir
Dawn	Dawn Popplewell

Directed by **John H. Newmeir**

CHARACTERS

Jones, 40s
Dawn, 40s
Hannah, 20s

The action of the play takes place in a psychiatric hospital

Time: the present

PRODUCTION NOTES

This is a powerful and challenging drama that needs a structured approach. As the Author, I have depressed the accelerator and now leave it to the producer to apply the brake wherever he or she deems appropriate. Control the arguing and conflict so that it does not exceed any great lengths. Pauses and softer moments must be found otherwise the actors may find the play too strenuous. Below are a few helpful tips.

Jones: Creating a character can sometimes prove difficult for any actor, no matter how experienced they may be. Therefore one might reason that creating *four* characters could be formidable. This rôle requires an extremely strong and competent actor to undertake and demonstrate the intricacies involved. Movement and body language would need to be explicit. Variation in pace, tempo and use of dramatic pause expressed, and emphasis, inflection and general vocal variation distinct. In the original production, Jones was given a Welsh accent with the actress using her own natural voice as Ivy Carr. The other voices were as per stage directions.

Hannah: Another difficult role owing to the fact that on the surface she appears to be the "normal" one of the three. Her dispassionate behaviour makes her the least obvious candidate to be the murderer. But this normality gives way occasionally to a threatening tone accompanied with intimidating actions that instils doubts and formulates scepticism within Jones's tormented mind.

Dawn: Easily the most transparent character of the three to interpret, and possibly the most enjoyable. Her simpering, imbecilic personality is clearly defined. Take care when she reveals her real identity towards the end that her transformation is total. She must display an *obvious* change in character, distinctive in both voice and mannerism.

Just a note of caution regarding the dossier placed on the table. Be mindful to depict the cover showing signs of regular usage. As for the contents, these should be extensive. Remember that Jones has been in the institution for almost nineteen years so she would have a fairly comprehensive dossier.

As for music, I have suggested *Windmills of Your Mind*. I found the words pertinent and the tune perfect in establishing an appropriate atmosphere. There are of course several versions of this song but I chose the recording by Johnny Mathis as being most apt.

J.H.N.

To my wife Ann whose belief and support
is my sole inspiration

SEMBLANCE OF MADNESS!

The female wing of a psychiatric hospital

UR, UC and UL represent separate "rooms". The downstage expanse denotes a hall or general recreational area with a chair and table (on which lies a dossier) DR. Other chairs etc. help set the locale with perhaps window flats standing either side

While the house lights dim, Windmills of Your Mind *begins playing through the darkness, helping to create the appropriate atmosphere. Approximately twenty seconds later the* CURTAIN *rises, and the music spills over while the stage remains in darkness, except for the backcloth which is draped and washed in a soft blue or red against the cyclorama. A few seconds and three separate areas become illuminated by secluded spots*

Three women stand with their backs towards the audience. Jones is UR (a notepad and pencil by her feet), dressed entirely in black, wearing slacks and a jumper. Her weathered face, short hair and strong voice all contribute to a masculine quality that makes her age indeterminable. Her strong beliefs, erratic temperament and unswerving passion for perfection, combined with an increasingly schizophrenic personality, help create an unpredictable and sinister character. Hannah is UC. She is modestly attractive, in her late forties to early fifties, and dressed sensibly considering the surroundings. Dawn is UL. Perhaps a generation less in age, her appearance is plain and drab and her clothes are dirty and stained. Slowly the UC and UL spots fade simultaneously, leaving Jones exposed, and as the music gives way, she turns with an unpleasant bearing

Jones (*to the audience*) I've been in this institution for almost nineteen years. I'm considered a senior member of the team and I'm respected and looked up to. I receive all sorts of perks such as food, money and free accommodation. They even allow me to run this theatre because I was once a professional actress. All I have to do in return is provide drama lessons to certain "chosen" individuals. I'm told it's therapeutic. (*She looks across*) For most that is.

Cross-fade to UL

Dawn (*to the audience*) Can't remember how long I was in here. Had a nervous breakdown last year, I couldn't seem to cope. Apparently I cried day and night over the least little thing. To all intents and purposes I drove everybody… (*she trails off*) well, you know. Fortunately, that's all behind me now—I'm fully recovered. I was afraid I'd lose my job, after all, not many employers are quick to sympathise. But they were marvellous— really understanding. They regarded it useful that I'd been a patient, so they've kept me on. As I've spent time on both sides of the fence, I know all about these two and what they're capable of. As a result they've placed me in here on "special duty".

Cross-fade to UC

Hannah (*to the audience*) I've only been here eighteen months, I'm fairly new to the job. All my family and friends found it hard to accept me coming to a place like this. Consequently, I haven't seen most of them for ages. Still, I'm happy enough and I get on with nearly everyone. Generally keep myself to myself. Mind you, Jones can be funny sometimes if you're not careful. I hear a pink slip's attached to her records. That means a history of violence. Got to supervise her closely, make sure she doesn't get the upper hand. Mind you, she's very clever.

Cross-fade to UR

Jones (*to the audience*) Don't listen to them, they're the patients—not me. It's obvious; one's a neurotic day-dreamer while the other's completely dispassionate. Definite symptoms of a psychopath. Oh yes, I said psychopath. You see, the authorities have been trying for some time to unmask a murderer thought to be here. (*She looks across at both of them*) Who knows?

Cross-fade to UL

Dawn (*to the audience*) Take no notice, I'm the trained psychiatric nurse around here. They do this all the time, it's a game they're playing and I have to go along with it if I'm to discover which of them is the killer. I'll pretend to be the whimpering fool to gain their confidence. Yes, they're the inmates … those two.

Cross-fade to UC

Hannah (*to the audience*) It's neither. *I'm* the psychotherapist assessor. It's a mouthful but at least they can't make any detrimental remarks like "trick cyclist" or "shrink". I organise these sessions to encourage communication. Although this one's special. One of those two committed murder and my job is to get the offender to openly admit it.

Cross-fade to UR

Jones (*to the audience*) For some of us, black and ebony can illustrate an objective finer than a blinding light. Within the stillness of the dark one can create and enrich an atmosphere so absorbing that it gives meaning and purpose. As a drama teacher, it is my task to delve into such places, and help expose those repressed memories and episodes that are invaluable when striving to reproduce and cultivate a dramatic character. After all, there is no substitute for one's own experiences of life.

Cross-fade to UL

Dawn (*to the audience; dancing*) I'm dancing to a packed auditorium. Dignitaries from near and far are gathered for this special performance. The orchestra begins emulating my every step with meticulous timing, as the follow spot never leaves my side. Finally, the applause is rapturous; I take ovation after ovation amid cries for encore. Fellow artistes join in with the acknowledgement of my mastery and professionalism.

Cross-fade to UC

Hannah (*to the audience*) Dancing? Huh, just an uncoordinated activity of noise and energy if you ask me—and it's aggravating. She's always up to something, I hear it all, these walls are paper-thin. Her life consists of just make-believe and day-dreams. She honestly *believes* she's cavorting around in there before a packed house at the Royal Albert Hall or Covent Garden. I'm convinced the word "realism" doesn't feature in her vocabulary. Escapism, that's what's needed around here. It's essential we create a diversion away from this humdrum environment, and there's no finer way than in drama. Helps to build up confidence—obtain some self-belief. Some people need to express themselves more thoroughly, learn to communicate with others. (*She looks across at Jones*) Heard some funny stories about this teacher. I had to think long and hard whether I'd accept her or not. Apparently she's unconventional, flying into sudden rages and shouting at the top of her voice for no reason. (*She contemplates*) But she *is* reputed to be the best.

Change to full general Lighting. Hannah looks at her watch and slowly crosses to the table, pondering at the dossier. Dawn recommences with her dancing

(*Shouting to Dawn*) Will you stop that infernal leaping around!

No response

You're doing it deliberately, aren't you?

Dawn No. (*She continues with her dancing*)

Hannah sits at the table and begins to peruse the dossier

Pause

Hannah (*tersely*) You really are most infuriating. I'm trying hard to concentrate.

Dawn And I'm dancing.

Hannah No, you're irritating!

Dawn It's occurred to me that I might be what they call … a "natural". I'm so full of dancing; it just feels really good. Perhaps that's my forte—to be a dancer. What kind though? … Modern? … No. How about tap? (*She attempts to tap dance*) Maybe not. Ballet! I could do ballet. (*She pirouettes*) "The Dying Swan". (*She crumples gracefully to the ground*) What do you think?

Hannah gives a contemptuous look and returns to her reading as Dawn moves DC, dancing and leaping around

Perhaps I should stick to acting. "Romeo, Romeo. Wherefore art thou, Romeo". Oh, yes, I can see it all now. Fame … fortune … flowers…

Hannah If only it was that easy. To dream and achieve, to imagine and obtain. No anguish … no hardship … no suffering.

Dawn I could join the Shakespeare Company and play the leading lady. I'd get to wear loads of fabulous costumes and kiss all those handsome fellahs.

Hannah You really are a day-dreamer, aren't you? Living in your own little world. Is that why you volunteered for these drama lessons? To fulfil all those fantasies constantly whirling around inside your brain.

Dawn You must be the same, otherwise you wouldn't be here, would you?

Hannah What else is there to do? Sit around all day watching telly and vegetate. No, thank you! At least this gives me something to do. (*She halts abruptly and glances at her watch*)

Dawn She's late. Maybe our teacher's not coming today.

Hannah She'll be here, she revels in it as much as you do.

Dawn I do enjoy it, the pretence that is. Don't like her moaning, though. She's always having a go at me. I don't think she likes me, do you?

Hannah Do I like you?

Dawn No. Do you think *she* likes me?

Hannah Does it matter?

Dawn She won't turn up because of me. She hates me.

Hannah Stop feeling sorry for yourself, you'll only get upset. She's late, that's all. I've told you, she'll be here.

Jones (*with a heavy Cockney accent*) Why don't you two just shut your gobs! You're getting on me piddling nerves, you're like a bleeding old married couple. Who gives a shit who likes who. Now pipe down and let met get some kip.

Hannah What did I say?

Dawn That's not Jones.

Hannah Yes, it is, she's playing at being someone else for the moment—and I know who.

Dawn Who?

Hannah Aggie.

Dawn Who's Aggie?

Hannah One of Jones's special friends. (*She points a finger to her head and whispers to Dawn*) She's schizo, suffers from a split personality, (*she points to the dossier*) says so right here.

Dawn What's that?

Hannah Some file I found lying on the table when I came in.

Dawn Oh Hannah, you shouldn't be reading it. What if it's private?

Hannah Of course it's private. It's been left here accidentally. Never mind that, listen to this. (*She reads from the dossier*) It says she has "schizophrenic tendencies resulting in frequent episodes of multi character manifestations, whereupon three separate personalities often materialise. The patient is convinced that the emergence of such characters are self-induced. Indeed, given her previous background of theatrical entertainment, we cannot at this period eradicate this possibility. However, studies have concluded" blah, blah, blah…

Dawn You shouldn't be doing that, Hannah. Anyway, I didn't understand a word of it. What does it mean?

Hannah It means she often appears as three other people beside herself. She's telling the doctors they're characters from her previous acting career, but they're saying it's all in her head.

Dawn You mean they don't know?

Hannah (*perusing the dossier*) I suppose they can't be sure. Good Lord! Do you realize she's been here nearly twenty years! You'd think they'd know after all that time, wouldn't you?

Dawn stares in disbelief at Jones's "room"

Dawn So she's not really who she says she is?

Hannah Only some of the time. Mostly she's herself.

Dawn (*confused*) I don't get this.

Hannah It's simple. The majority of the time Jones is Jones, but every now and then she pretends to be someone else.

Dawn Does she do it deliberately?

Hannah Well, that's what Jones says, but the doctors think otherwise, they say she can't help it. They think it's an illness with her—something she can't control. That's why she's here.

Dawn So who's in her room now?

Hannah Wait a minute, that was on a previous page. (*She turns back a page*) Here it is. Aggie, a docker's wife from Poplar.

Dawn How can you tell?

Hannah Because she's the only one with a Cockney accent. It can't be any of the others because they're … let's see… (*She looks at the dossier*) Dame Sadie Kent, a theatrical impresario from Mortlake, she defiantly wouldn't speak like that, and then there's Ivy Carr, journalist and part-time newsreader from Friern Barnet. Now, they most certainly have to pronounce their Hs, so she's out. So you see, it has to be Aggie. I'll tell you what, she gets around, that's for sure.

Jones For Christ sake! The pair of you are giving my arse an 'eadache. Do me a favour an' give your sodding traps a rest.

Hannah You're not in a very good mood today, are you—Aggie?

Jones Piss off!

Dawn Charming. So what do we do now?

Hannah Wait. What else can we do? (*She flicks hastily through the remainder of the dossier*) Funny, there's no pink slip or any mention of violence.

Dawn (*feeling dejected*) Doesn't sound as if we're going to do anything today. I'm going back to my room. (*She moves* UL *to her "room", sitting cross-legged with her back towards the audience*)

Hannah looks towards Jones's "room", closes the dossier and crosses to Jones

Hannah Hallo, Aggie. It is Aggie, isn't it?

Jones (*coldly*) Clear off.

Hannah Just thought you might know where Jones is, she's supposed to be giving a drama lesson in the main hall.

No response

Fair enough. I'll go back to my room and we'll call it a day. (*She starts to go*)

Half turning, Jones gives out a piercing laugh over her shoulder

Jones (*as herself*) You're so gullible. There's no such person as Aggie, she doesn't exist. It was me *acting*.

Hannah So where does Aggie come from?

Jones (*facing Hannah*) Somebody I once created. Used her in a play at the Garrick Theatre, ran for over three years. Aggie Warbourn was her full name. Docker's wife and proud of it—great character. (*As Aggie*) Never went short for nuffing when my 'Arry was working. 'Alf inched everything he did. Weren't nuffing 'e couldn't swipe off them ships. 'Course, it's all been elbowed now, the docks I mean. Closed it all down—rotten gits! (*Sitting up, she looks beyond Hannah and reverts back to her normal voice*) Where's the other one? The snivelling simpleton.

Hannah Dawn? Gone back to her room sulking.

Jones (*moving* DC) There's always something with her. So, what's she upset about now?

Hannah She's persuaded herself you're not teaching today ... are you?

Jones Why should I? She never pays any attention, it's just a laugh to her. She can't act. Come to think of it, she can't do anything except wind me up. She's useless. A total waste of space.

Hannah Have you any idea how much she looks forward to these lessons? Do you know she has a chart in her room where she ticks off the hours starting from when the previous lesson ended? And on the actual day she counts down the minutes, the *minutes* mind you, from when she first gets up. She might be useless, but she's keen.

Jones immediately adopts the character of Dame Sadie Kent, a cultured and refined woman speaking with eloquence and fluency

Jones Whatever antics she elects to amuse herself with, they are of little consequence to me. Needless to say she is an expendable statistic that fortunately for her I choose to endure—for now.

Hannah Well, that wasn't Aggie, that's for sure. So who's she suppose to be?

Jones (*as herself*) That, my friend, is Sadie. Dame Sadie Kent, theatrical impresario of the highest order, now residing in Mortlake. She first came to prominence at the Aldwych in a play purposefully scripted for me. I'm very fond of her and she always seems to be on hand whenever I get into difficulty with my teachings. An eminent mentor.

Hannah So, is that what you think about me? An expendable statistic?

Jones You're slightly different. Haven't worked you out yet. You're not as stupid as she is, it's almost as if you don't belong in a place like this. I'm trying hard to make up my mind whether you're smarter than you let on, or you're a very good actor—or liar, they're very often the same thing. Which is it?

Hannah Maybe I'm all three. A smart actor who lies a lot.

Jones True. Or perhaps a lying actor who's really not very smart at all.

Hannah Well, I'll leave it up you to choose. Maybe Sadie'll help you make up your mind.

Jones No hurry, I'll find out in time. (*She crosses* C) Now you'd better get dozy balls before she floods the entire wing with her tears. (*She picks up the table and moves it across, resting it down at an angle slightly off centre*)

Hannah places the dossier in her "room"

Hannah (*calling off*) Dawn! Jones is here, we're ready to start. (*To Jones*) What about you?

Jones selects a nearby chair and places it behind the table

Jones Am I nuts, you mean? Suppose I must be. Why else would I remain in here for nineteen years. After all, I'm not committed. (*She sits down and puts both feet on the table, folding her arms behind her back and stretches back*)

Hannah looks at her amazed

That's shook you, hasn't it? No, I could walk out of here anytime I wanted to. You can't, can you?

Hannah Tell me about Aggie and Sadie.

Jones I've already told you all about them. What else do you want to know?

Hannah I was just wondering if they're real or not. You know the sort of thing, is the show one big act or the act one big show.

Jones Very clever. You tell me, Miss Smarty Pants.

Hannah (*with a cutting grin*) As you just said, "there's no hurry, I'll find out in time".

Jones (*flippantly*) Touché.

Dawn skips DC with excitement

Dawn What shall we do, then? Any suggestions? (*She gyrates*)
    How about dancing?

*Jumping up, Jones takes on a sinister pose, her face distorting and
eyes bulging. She pitches forward a few steps towards Dawn with
rage, then suddenly stops, appears to recompose herself, and then
adopts the character of Dame Sadie Kent, which unsettles Hannah
who is looking on*

Jones (*curtly as Sadie Kent*) I find dancing to be the most profane
    growth of exhibitionism. It debases and degrades the very concept
    of dramatic art. It has no function here. Should you wish to
    continue as my pupil, then you would be well advised to discover
    and express the masters of verse. To read the utterance and
    phrases of wordsmiths such as Ibsen and Shaw, Williams and
    Coward. Not forgetting the great bard himself, William
    Shakespeare.
Dawn (*to Hannah*) What did she say?
Hannah Stop dancing and start reading. And I agree with her, if it'll
    stop all that racket you keep making in your room. Constantly
    jumping up and down, it's enough to test the patience of a saint.
    Maybe I'll get some peace.
Dawn Why? What's wrong with dancing? It's a form of expression.

Spinning round, Jones moves effortlessly back into her normal self

Jones (*nastily as herself*) How would you know about expressing
    yourself?
Dawn Because I read it somewhere, that's how.
Hannah Where? The loo walls.
Dawn No, in a magazine, if you must know. I found it lying by the
    bin in the TV room. Didn't have anyone's name on it, so I took it.
Hannah That's thieving. Just because it didn't have anyone's name
    on it doesn't make it yours. I hope you've put it back.
Dawn Why should I? Haven't finished with it yet. Besides, I've had
    plenty of things taken in this place and no-one's ever brought
    mine back.

Hannah You've got nothing worth stealing.

Dawn Not now, but I did have.

Jones So what is it you want to express?

Dawn Don't know, the magazine never said. But I enjoy doing it, though.

Jones (*flaring*) Are you taking the piss?

Dawn No!

Jones hurls herself forward

Jones (*grabbing Dawn's clothes*) Because if you are…

Dawn (*quickly*) I'm not … honest.

Hannah (*getting between them*) What's the matter with you, Jones? Are you trying to get us all in trouble? For God's sake, let her go before someone comes in and we get thrown back to our rooms. If they catch us fighting, there'll be no more drama lessons, and you know what that means, don't you? Bloody supervised telly watching. Now let her go.

Jones begrudgingly releases Dawn and moves away. Pause

Jones I've come to a decision. (*She points at Dawn*) I want you out.

Dawn (*alarmed*) What!!

Jones You heard.

Hannah (*concerned*) You can't do that!

Jones Yes I can, because I'm the teacher—I'm in charge. They gave me a free hand, remember. (*As Aggie*) If I don't want 'er then I don't have to keep 'er. And I don't bloody want 'er, see? So there.

Dawn (*desperately*) But I *want* to stay here.

Jones Well, I don't want *you*, it's as simple as that. Now piss off!

Dawn What have I done wrong?

Jones Everyfing.

Hannah You can't be serious.

Jones (*as herself*) I'm perfectly serious. In fact, I should've got rid of her after the first lesson.

Dawn Hannah, help me. Stop her—make her let me stay.

Hannah For God's sake! Look at her!
Jones Keep out of this, you!
Hannah Just tell me why?

In a sudden torrent of rage, Jones storms towards her, spitting hatefully

Jones Because she's repulsive and repugnant and stinks to high heaven. Look at the state of her.

Dawn shelters behind Hannah

It's disgusting! Besides which she can't act, speak, stand or project and (*to Dawn*) despite what you think, (*shouting in her face*) you can't even bloody dance properly.

The ferocity of her words cause Dawn to break down

Hannah That's uncalled for.
Jones (*ignoring her*) You lack ambition, commitment, passion and above all talent. Not to mention cleanliness.
Dawn (*through her tears*) I don't. (*She flees to the table and throws herself down, sobbing uncontrollably*)
Hannah Why are you being like this? Because she was dancing?
Jones Is that what you call it, eh?
Hannah You can't go round throwing someone out just because they like something you don't. Even the trustees won't back you on that one.
Jones But I can if she's a thief, that's against the rules. You heard yourself, she admitted to taking that magazine which didn't belong to her, didn't you? You can't deny that.
Hannah There's absolutely no malice with her, she just lives in a world of make-believe, that's all. Her own private world of fantasy. She probably made the whole thing up.
Jones (*to Dawn*) Did you? Did you make it up or did you take it? Be honest now.
Dawn It was lying in the bin, there was nobody else in the room.

Hannah There you are, it'd been thrown away. Her only crime is she's a day-dreamer.

Jones She's an idiot!

Hannah Now you're out of order, Jones. We don't say that about anybody around here.

Jones Oh, it's sanctimonious Hannah now, is it?

Hannah You're only picking on her because she can't defend herself, aren't you? You just take back what you said.

Jones Or…?

Hannah (*towards her*) Just take it back, Jones. I'm warning you.

Jones What are you? Everyone's champion? Crusading for the worthy cause. Only she's not, is she? Worthy I mean. You complained yourself about the disturbance.

Hannah What disturbance?

Jones Earlier, when I was still in my room. Didn't think I heard, did you? You was trying to read something, only she was jumping up and down. Called her irritating, didn't you? You couldn't concentrate because your mind was distracted. You can't afford that on stage, and you shouldn't entertain those that create it either, they're bad for you. Like her.

Dawn (*sobbing*) I didn't mean it, honestly.

Hannah Don't you try twisting this around to me.

Jones She knows the rules. Concentration was broken, that's distraction. She has to learn I won't condone it. I'm very selective as to the standard I demand from my pupils. I expect more from them after one day than they expect from themselves after one year.

Hannah Then your standards are too high. This isn't some palatial dramatic academy, it's a psychiatric hospital and you're supposed to be helping the patients, not aggravating them.

Jones I'm very sincere about what I do regardless of where it is.

Hannah So is she if you'd let her. Just give her a chance.

Jones She's had loads of chances.

Hannah If she goes… I go! Then you'll have no-one left to boss around, will you? No more pupils, no more lessons … in short, no more class.

Jones (*frivolously*) Hannah the lion-hearted.

Hannah She needs to be wanted. All I'm saying is try to understand her.

Jones Give me one good reason why I should waste my time?

Hannah Because you're her teacher.

Jones Was. Was her teacher. Not anymore. She's too distracting—too disruptive.

Hannah Everything in life is either distracting or disruptive.

Jones Not in the theatre.

Hannah (*desperately*) That's no exception. What about when someone coughs in an audience or rattles a sweet packet, aren't they being distracting? And the ones that arrive late after the show has started, isn't that disruptive?

Jones (*face to face with Hannah*) Those type of disturbances come from the public who often don't know any better. Cast members and backstage crews *do* know better. It's unprofessional. I won't have that in my class…

Hannah So you're just going to chuck her out.

Jones There's no finer education than a practical one. She'll know better next time.

Hannah You can't do this to her. There won't be a next time, not in here and you know that. If she's turned out of this therapy class for being a hindrance you know what corrective measures they'll take.

Jones (*dismissively*) Not my problem. (*To Dawn*) Now get out!

Hannah Stay where you are.

Dawn (*rising*) But I want to remain here with you. I couldn't stand…

Jones (*ranting*) I said *get out*!!

Dawn (*pleading*) I'll never dance any more… I swear on my life. (*She crosses her heart with her finger*) Cross my heart and hope to die.

Hannah Don't do this, Jones.

Dawn Please, Jones … *please*.

Jones rushes over to Dawn, pushing her violently to the ground

Jones (*shouting*) I said GET OUT!!!

Hannah slaps Jones hard across the face, bringing her to an abrupt halt. There is an uneasy pause for a second or two and then Jones crosses to her "room". Hannah helps Dawn to her feet and then to her "room". Cross-fade to a spot UL

Hannah (*to the audience*) She's fast becoming unstable. Her irrational behaviour and sudden bursts of temper are bordering on the precarious. Her nonconformity is becoming less and less isolated. There was no logical reason for what just happened, a completely unprovoked attack. Poor Dawn, she so looks forward to these sessions. Something's got to be done about Jones. She frightens me.

Dawn (*to the audience*) I love coming here, pretending to be other people. I can be anyone I want, like a queen or a glamorous film star, or even a famous singer. It gives me a window to climb through when I need to escape from the routines and pressures of life. Can't be a dancer though, Jones won't allow it. She's paranoid about any form of dancing. I wish Hannah was the teacher, I get on with her. But Jones scares me.

Cross-fade to UR

Jones (*to the audience*) Forgive my little eccentricities, but I had to capture their attention and focus their minds. It's a vital lesson they've had to learn. You see, a truly great performance can only be accomplished with concentration and dedication. Both points they lack. Dedication is a virtue in the theatre, indeed elsewhere as well. It's what's needed but often missing. Without it you're nothing… I'm nothing … we're all nothing.

Change to full general Lighting. Picking up the note pad and pencil, Jones crosses over to Dawn and Hannah as Ivy Carr, the journalist. An enthusiastic woman with an eye for a story

Excuse me, I'm Ivy Carr from the *Gazette*. I understand there's been an incident recently inside the hospital. Would you care to make a comment?

No response

Is it right that some of the inmates have been fighting?

No response

Can you give me the names of those that took part in the riot?

No response

Were you involved yourself? Look, I've got a deadline to meet and this is a potentially explosive story. I can see the headlines now… "Girls in local asylum fight over…" What were you fighting over? Conditions…? Men…? Other women…?

Hannah Yes, other women. No, change that, just one in particular. One very nasty, egotistical, jumped-up tart!

Jones (*scribbling*) This is gonna be great. An emotional angle. Who is this supercilious female?

Hannah Calls herself by her surname—*Jones*. I think you'll find you might know her very well.

Jones (*shrugging her shoulders*) Common name. Anyone else involved?

No reply

Come on, don't stop there. What was it about? Lesbian jealousy … three in a bed … new girl on the block. (*Disappointedly*) Don't tell me it was just a lovers tiff.

Hannah stares at her in disbelief

Can I have your name—for the paper. I won't print it, if you don't want. Have to show my editor the source.

Hannah (*moving* DL *disinterestedly*) Get lost!

Jones That's very nice, isn't it? I'm only trying to do my job.

Dawn (*moving forward dubiously*) I … er … I know her name. It's Hannah. Hannah Corbin.

Jones I know perfectly well who she is, and why she's here. I covered the trial at Snaresbrook for the local rag. It actually gave me the break I needed. Got me noticed by the big boys.

Dawn Big boys? (*She looks at her blankly*)

Jones Dailies. As in newspapers—oh, never mind.

Dawn I'm Dawn Bishop. I'm a danc…

Jones stiffens with horror in anticipation, then quickly relaxes

Actually I'm learning to be an actor … or was. That's what caused all the trouble in the first place. Jones threw me out.

Throwing the pad and pencil across towards her "room", Jones bursts into her piercing, almost evil laugh

Jones (*as herself*) What a performance. Your faces, you ought to see them, they're a picture.

Dawn What's so funny?

Jones You … both of you. I've been stringing the pair of you along for ages. Slowly reeling you in. You've been completely fooled.

Hannah turns to listen

You believed every word … thoroughly taken in. Now that's acting.

Hannah (*incredulously*) All this was acting?

Jones (*pleased with herself*) Unquestionably.

Hannah You mean you set the whole thing up.

Jones (*matter-of-factly*) Of course. (*As Sadie Kent*) You see, acting is the study of speech inflection and pitch, blended with its applicable action or gesture it becomes a science. Combine this science with one's own intimate experiences of life, and cultivate this craft to be replicated or mimeographed when required, and you have effectively mastered the technique of skilled and controlled acting. (*As Aggie*) Never mind about all that old crap. Good, weren't I? You never 'ad a clue.

Dawn (*bemused*) You make it sound like a recipe. Mix this, blend that, bring something else to the boil and serve it all together.

Jones (*to Hannah*) Wha' do you fink, girl? I know you've got your lug 'oles opened, I can 'ear the lobes flapping around from 'ere.

Hannah (*sardonically*) Very convincing.

Jones (*as herself*) You mean skilful.

Dawn (*with sudden realization*) You … you mean it was just pretending.

Jones Quick, isn't she?

Dawn (*excitedly*) Then I can stay.

Awkward pause

Hannah Well—can she?

Jones (*to Dawn*) Do you promise commitment?

Dawn looks apprehensively towards Hannah who returns a reassuring nod as she crosses c

Dawn (*thrilled*) Yes.

Pause to consider

Jones (*relenting*) Very well.

Dawn moves eagerly towards her

Dawn Brilliant. I'll never play you up or do anything to make you wild with me ever again. (*She crosses to Hannah and hugs her tightly*) Thanks a lot, Hannah. You were marvellous.

Jones I think you should be thanking me. After all, I'm the one who's yielding here.

As Dawn moves across, Jones deliberately turns her back

Dawn Oh, yes, sorry, Jones. Are you sure you don't mind?

Jones (*turning back with sudden rage*) Mind? I do mind. I mind
   very much.
Dawn (*shocked*) But…

Switching quickly to a broad smile, Jones places an arm around her

Jones (*as Sadie Kent*) But I'll make an exception in this instance,
   providing there is no repetition or exploitation.
Dawn I promise.
Jones (*as herself*) Good. (*She pushes Dawn away*) Then fetch
   another chair and we'll continue with the lesson.

Hannah catches hold of Dawn's arm as she starts to move

Hannah (*to Jones*) Please.

There is an uneasy pause as the two stare hard at each other

   I said "please".
Jones (*with a forced smile*) Please.

Hannah releases Dawn's arm. Dawn gazes around

Hannah (*pointing*) There's one over there.

Dawn scurries over and retrieves the chair

   (*Quietly to Jones*) You were rude.
Jones On the contrary, she was rude for disturbing my rehearsal in
   the first place.

*Hannah slowly shakes her head incredulously as Dawn returns
with the chair and places it L of the table*

   (*To Dawn*) I bet you'd like to act just like me … eh, Dawn?
Dawn You know I would, if you think I'm good enough.
Jones That depends on you. Do you think you are?

Dawn (*seeking confidence from Hannah*) I don't really know …
   probably.

Jones What about you, Hannah? Can you act or are you just smart?

Hannah Still haven't worked it out, then.

Jones OK. Let's find out once and for all, shall we? (*She repositions the table* DC) Sit down—the pair of you.

Dawn sits behind the table, Hannah places herself on the left. Using the complete DC *area, Jones begins in a calm, controlled voice*

   We'll begin with a little improvisation. I want you both to imagine that you're inside a police station, being questioned.

Hannah What about?

Jones You choose a subject … better still, how about Dawn?

Dawn Er … don't know. Give me a clue.

Jones Select a crime for which you could be interviewed for—a serious crime.

Dawn Pickpocketing.

Jones (*with controlled patience*) No, try a bit harder, Dawn. Remember commitment. I said a serious crime.

Dawn House breaking.

Jones Better. But aim for something a little higher, something a little more grave.

Dawn Armed robbery, then.

Jones Higher still.

Pause while Dawn thinks

   Come on, Dawn, it isn't that difficult. There's plenty to choose from.

Dawn (*becoming worried*) I can't think of any.

Jones Yes, you can. Concentrate.

Dawn (*panicking*) I can't! My mind's gone blank.

Jones (*raising her voice*) Try, Dawn. Think harder. What's more evil, more cold-blooded than any crime imaginable? What's the foulest and most despicable act you can commit against a fellow human being? What is it, Dawn? What is it? Tell me, Dawn. Tell me ... tell me, damn you.

Dawn (*shouting*) Murder!

Jones That's right—murder! You can relate to that, can't you, Dawn?

Pause

This is DCI Jones along with WPC Corbin, the time is (*she looks at her watch*) oh nine forty-seven, and we are interviewing Dawn Bishop, also present is... (*She pauses, a wry smile across her face*) Oh dear, you haven't got a solicitor—never mind. For the purpose of the tape, the suspect has declined legal representation. Her rights have been read to her which she has acknowledged. Tell me, Miss Bishop. Did you commit this evil and despicable murder?

Dawn No!

Jones But we have several witnesses who claim they saw you at the scene of the crime, holding the blood-stained weapon. Also, a piece of your torn blouse was firmly clenched in the victim's hand, and your fingerprints were everywhere. You had motive and opportunity. We've been told how she treated you ... goaded you ... insulted and embarrassed you. All of a sudden it became too much, you couldn't handle it any more, something inside just snapped. You don't know where or how but suddenly there was a knife in your hands and the victim was in front of you laughing, taunting, calling you names. So you stabbed her, only it wasn't just once, was it? That wasn't enough for you, you couldn't feel satisfied or avenged until you struck her at least thirty times. Once you started, you couldn't stop, couldn't control yourself. You had to keep going, something deep down urged you on and on and on. That little voice inside your head kept saying revenge! ... revenge! ... revenge!

Dawn (*breaking down*) No, no, no.

Hannah (*sternly*) That's enough! You're going too far.

Jones It's role-play.

Hannah (*rising*) It's vindictive. You're overstepping the mark—
   now back off!

*Jones reluctantly moves away and Hannah retakes her seat,
comforting Dawn. As matters calm down, Dawn's crying slowly
eases. Pause*

Jones Tell me what you're thinking, Dawn?
Dawn I can't.
Jones You use that word a lot, don't you, Dawn? In reality it's just
   an excuse, isn't it? There is no such word as can't. Explain to me
   how you feel right now.
Dawn (*quietly*) Scared.
Jones Sorry?
Dawn (*louder*) Scared.
Jones I can't hear you. Fill those lungs, Dawn—project that voice.
Dawn (*shouting*) I said I'm scared.
Jones (*triumphantly*) Ah, at last an emotion and said with
   compassion. (*As Sadie Kent*) Fasten it into the memory to be
   summoned when necessitated on stage. (*As herself*) Now, tell me
   what you're scared of, Dawn?

No response

   Is it love?

Dawn shakes her head

   Sorrow…?

Again Dawn shakes her head

   Envy…?

Dawn continues shaking her head

   Anger…?

Dawn tenses

You're angry? What at?

Hannah I would've thought that was obvious.

Jones Oh?

Hannah It's a defence because she's scared—of *you*!

Jones Is that right, Dawn? Are you scared of me?

No reply

Hannah You can see it written on her face. What sort of teacher are you?

Jones The best, that's why I think there's something else that scares her. Something she's not telling us. What is, Dawn? What's troubling you? (*Towards Dawn*) Tell me your thoughts. Reveal that inner mind. Remember, memory must be total and accurate or else it becomes extremely dangerous to the thespian.

Dawn starts crying slowly at first and then sobbing, her complete body shaking with the ferocity

Why are you crying, Dawn—tell me why you're crying at this precise moment?

Jones and Hannah exchange glances

Drama is nothing more than a recollection from your own framework of life. The intensity and suspense from one's own background. You're crying because you're beginning to perceive all those trials and tribulations you've encountered, aren't you, Dawn? In your mind you're conjuring up some terrible incident or ordeal you've suffered, aren't you? Come on, Dawn, don't be shy. Stop crying and tell us all about it. Get it out of your system. Let it go and be free.

Hannah Leave her alone.

Jones But she wants to tell me, don't you, Dawn?

Hannah (*rising*) I said leave her alone.

Jones (*severely*) Sit down!

Hannah Who are you…

Jones (*screaming*) I said sit down!! I've had enough of your interfering.

Hannah (*sitting*) I'll report you for this.

Jones Come on, Dawn, I want to hear your darkest secret. Those things you've never talked about before. You can't have inhibitions in drama. Think of all those parts that would be offered to you if we could break through this barrier you're putting up. All you have to do is be honest and open. Confide in us and get everything off your chest. You'll be a better actress for it.

Dawn (*sobbing*) I… I… I just can't.

Jones suddenly explodes into an unforeseen rage

Jones (*banging the table*) You promised me. You promised commitment if I let you stay! You lied to me!

Dawn I didn't mean to.

Jones (*shouting*) Liar liar pants on fire!

Hannah (*rising*) Why don't you stop bullying her, that's all you've been doing since we came here tonight. She's doing her best.

Jones Then it's not good enough!

Hannah Can't you see she's highly-strung? You're not helping her, you're driving her towards another nervous breakdown.

Jones (*as Aggie*) She's a lying two-faced mare! She knew bloody well she wouldn't keep that promise when she made it.

Hannah Because it didn't mean anything. It was an act, you said so yourself.

Jones What d'you know, you turned-up old trollop? Always gotta stick your nose in where it don't belong, ain't yer?

Hannah You're only resorting to insults because you know I'm right.

Just as suddenly as her rage exploded, Jones takes on a composed presence, yet again dramatically creating a personality transformation

Jones (*as Sadie Kent*) You jest, of course. The piece of skilful acting
you refer to was actually prior to the promise undertaken. I was
entirely earnest about the commitment and dedication. For without
it one is not in command, therefore one encourages scepticism ...
indecision ... uncertainty ... misgivings ... apprehension. You
have to be more definite. Acting is to be in control at every instant.
You have to govern, domineer, dominate and master one's every
encounter and feeling. Supervise each thought and movement.
You have to think and be more positive.

Hannah That's as may be but she can't, she's not made that way.

Jones (*as herself*) And why isn't she? I'll tell you why, because you
won't let her breathe, you're always there to protect her. You
won't let her stand on her own two feet.

Hannah Because she's weak.

Jones Then let her get strong.

Hannah I wish I could ... look at her? Take a good look! She'll
never be strong. You only have to raise your voice and the tears
stream down her face. She's a complete bundle of nerves.

Jones But you're not, are you? You're strong and powerful. You
won't let her think for herself, you do it all for her.

Hannah Somebody has to.

Jones So you've appointed yourself, have you?

Hannah Who else is there ... you?

Jones That's exactly right. I could help her get strong, help her to
stand on her own two feet ... think for herself and become more
self-assured.

Hannah By bullying and abusing her? Is that what your schoolroom
tactics are based around?

Jones They're designed to bring out the best in people. To induce
confidence and purpose in what they say and do.

Hannah Does she look confident and full of purpose to you?

Jones That's because of your incessant interference.

Hannah No! It's because you don't bloody know what you're
doing! You're a fake! ... an impostor! ... a charlatan! You know
no more about drama than Joe Bloggs! These characters you keep
coming up with are all in your head.

Jones And what's in your head, eh?

Hannah None of your business.

Jones Oh, but that's where you're wrong. It is my business. It's my business to know what all my students think. What makes them tick.

Hannah If you're so clever, you tell me.

Jones Domination! That's what you're all about, Hannah Corbin. You're manipulative. You like to control people without them being aware. That's why you keep challenging me, isn't it? Because I won't let you, I resist your overtones.

Hannah You're just...

Jones Mad! Is that what you was going to say?

Hannah ...Ridiculous.

Jones Maybe we are—mad that is. Maybe we're just a semblance of madness.

Hannah Don't call me by that word, I don't like it.

Jones What word? Oh, you mean "*mad*".

Hannah I told you, don't say that.

Jones Why Hannah? What's wrong with "*mad*".

Hannah It's humiliating.

Moving towards her, Jones begins taunting Hannah

Jones Mad! ... mad! ... mad! ... mad! ... mad! ... mad! ... mad!

Hannah (*covering her ears*) Stop it! Stop it!! (*Working herself into a frenzy, she begins leaping around in bizarre fashion, completely out of control*)

Jones Mad! ... mad! ... mad! ... mad! ... mad! ... mad! ... mad!

Dawn (*jumping up*) Leave her alone!

Jones (*towards Dawn*) Mad! ... mad! ... mad! ... mad!

Dawn (*wildly*) I can't take any more! I can't take any more!!

Jones moves in close to Dawn, shouting into her face

Jones Mad! ... mad! ... mad! ... mad! ... mad! ... mad! ... mad!...

Dawn suddenly grabs hold of Jones, dragging her to the floor

Dawn You bitch! I'll bloody kill you! (*She places both hands around Jones's throat in an attempt to throttle her*)
Jones (*gasping for breath*) Get her off! Get her off!

At first, Hannah is transfixed, caught between surprise and approval. Finally, and in the nick of time, she comes to her senses, rushes over and, seizing Dawn around the neck while thrusting Dawn's arm up her back, she drags her off

Hannah Let go, Dawn … it's all over. Let her go!
Dawn (*struggling*) I'll kill her! I'll kill her!
Hannah Calm down, Dawn. It's over.

Gradually, the struggling subsides as Dawn begins sobbing

(*To Jones*) Satisfied? (*She relinquishes her hold*)

Dawn slowly sinks on to her knees. Jones pulls herself up, sitting L of the table, rubbing her neck

Dawn (*to the audience*) All I ever wanted to do was dance, but she wouldn't let me. Told me that it was all nonsense, that nobody in their right minds danced. It was just for losers and people unfit to act. She said if I wanted to be famous I should concentrate on acting. And I did want to be somebody … anybody, so very badly. But I couldn't do anything right. No matter what I did or how hard I worked, or even how many times I practised, it was never good enough for her. So my mind started wandering. Tunes kept coming into my head. Without realizing, I felt my fingers and toes tapping, the whole thing was giving me a thrill—it was exciting. Before I knew what I was doing, I found myself jigging around before and after her lessons, and sometimes even during lessons, when I wasn't needed for a particular scene. That's when it happened. She started hollering and shouting abuse at me. She went absolutely berserk! Told me I couldn't dance, that I was pathetic. Claimed she always referred to me with the others behind my back as "silly Dawn the useless imbecile". She was showing me up in front of everyone, I told her to stop but she wouldn't, she kept on and on and on. So I threatened her, all I wanted to do was to make her stop—but she wouldn't. I begged her to stop, promised I'd never dance again but she kept on shouting and shouting in my face. So I...

Hannah ...So you killed her?

Dawn (*offended*) No! I couldn't do that. It's true I lost my temper and I wanted to hurt her—but I couldn't.

Jones (*slowly*) Just like Claire. After two years in my class she couldn't even express that one simple emotion. Totally useless she was. Cost me everything I had, everything I'd worked for.

Realizing Jones is about to confess, Hannah's character changes, as she pushes for the final answers

Hannah Who's Claire?

Jones You must have read about her? An absolutely worthless article who served no purpose at all. She was ineffectual and entirely unproductive. She deserved to die.

Hannah No-one deserves to die.

Jones Well, she did. (*She points*) And so does she, they're both the same.

Hannah That's where you're wrong, Jones.

Jones Am I? She can't act.

Hannah On the contrary, she's acted superbly. Tell her, Dawn.

Dawn's character also changes. Her voice and body language becoming more severe and authoritative

Dawn (*rising to her feet*) My name's not really Dawn Bishop, it's Helen Forbes. And I'm not an inpatient, I'm actually a trained psychiatric nurse.

Hannah She was brought in to help me. This is her first assignment.

Jones But she was in here last year, I saw her myself.

Dawn I did have a breakdown, that bit's true. But I'm fully recovered now and back at work.

Hannah That's why I got her to assist me. Because you already

knew her, you'd accept me easier. She took on the role of Claire
under a different name to force you out into the open. We had to
discover the truth, Jones, that way we can help you.

Jones You tricked me.

Hannah You tricked yourself.

Jones Well, I only said she deserved to die, not that I did it. So you're
not that clever, are you?

Hannah You thought Dawn was a fool when in fact she was only
acting. It was the same with Claire, wasn't it? Only she acted the
fool because she lacked confidence. Dancing was her way of
dealing with it. If you'd shown her more faith and helped her,
maybe, just maybe, things would have turned out different. All
she ever wanted was to be someone, she was a dreamer. Claire
died because she dared to stand up to all your innuendoes and
insults. Your pride wouldn't allow this ineffective, feeble buffoon
to challenge your authority or integrity, so you killed her, didn't
you?

*The impact of Hannah's words has visibly affected Jones. She
slumps into the chair behind the table, her body shaking and face
ashen. Eventually, she composes herself, sits up straight and facing
out, begins as if reading a news bulletin. Cross-fade to a pool of light
spilling over the table*

Jones (*to the audience as Ivy Carr*) Good evening. The main story
tonight. Earlier today two psychiatric nurses from a local state-
run hospital were accused of duping an inmate into believing they
were fellow patients. It is believed they obtained the confidence
of the patient in order to extract a confession. The nurses claim
they were acting under direct instructions from the Home Office.
The Prime Minister has ordered an immediate inquiry.

*Hannah and Dawn step closer into the light, one at each of Jones's
shoulders. Simultaneously they look to each other and then down at
Jones*

The inmate, who for legal reason cannot be named, is thought to be the former West End stage actress Margaret Jones, who was believed to be responsible for the killing of her former pupil Claire Wallace almost twenty years ago. The case never came to trial because the former star volunteered herself for psychiatric evaluation which has been ongoing ever since. The police have never sought any other suspect in connection with the murder although the case still remains open. Earlier our legal correspondent caught up with some of Miss Jones's former students. (*She rises and transposes into Sadie Kent*) Look, I'm afraid I have no comment to offer. I last saw Margaret Jones approximately two weeks before the sordid episode came to light. As a former member of the same class what I will say is that Claire Wallace was a complete distraction. (*She moves to the front of the table*) She was the reason I and the rest of the course stopped attending. Miss Jones did become bitter after seeing her following dwindle from over thirty to just one. To my mind, she was a saint to persevere with her as long as she did. Whether or not she was ever innocent or guilty does not in the least interest me. Now kindly leave me alone before I set the dogs on you. (*She draws the chair L of the table, places it in front and sits astride. Leaning forward, she rests on the chair's back. Her personality converts once again—this time to Aggie*) Bleedin' good, ain't it? Soon know who your friends are when the shit 'its the fan. No-one ever came forward for the old dragon. Luckily, as it turned out, they didn't 'ave to. Mind you, that young bird what's-her-name, *was* a pest. Always larking about she was. Drove the old turd batty. Couldn't help feeling sorry for 'er though, Jones I mean. Just went a bit do-lally, I suppose. It could 'appen to any of us. 'Course, I don't 'old with no killing. Fieving's a different matter. My 'Arry did plenty of that in his time, but 'e never 'urt no-one. Not physically that is. As to the murder, personally I fink she done it… What do you fink? (*She stares hard at the audience for a second and then leans back with a smug smile beaming across her face*)

The CURTAIN *falls*

FURNITURE AND PROPERTY LIST

On stage: 3 chairs
Table. *On it*: dossier
Window flats (optional)
Note pad
Pencil

Personal: **Hannah:** watch
Jones: watch
Dawn: watch

LIGHTING PLOT

Property fittings required: nil
1 interior. The same throughout

To open: Soft blue or red on backcloth

Cue 1   Following twenty seconds of music   (Page 1)
           Bring up spots DR, DL, *and* UC; *a few seconds*
              later, slowly fade out UC *and* UL *spots*

Cue 2   **Jones**: "For most that is."   (Page 2)
           Cross-fade to spot UL

Cue 3   **Dawn**: "…placed me in here on special duty."   (Page 2)
           Cross-fade to spot UC

Cue 4   **Hannah**: "Mind you, she's very clever."   (Page 2)
           Cross-fade to spot UR

Cue 5   **Jones**: "Who knows?"   (Page 3)
           Cross-fade to spot UL

Cue 6   **Dawn**: "…they're the inmates … those two."   (Page 3)
           Cross-fade to spot UC

Cue 7   **Hannah**: "…the offender to openly admit it."   (Page 3)
           Cross-fade to spot UR

Cue 8   **Jones**: "…one's own experiences of life."   (Page 3)
           Cross-fade to spot UL

Cue 9	**Dawn**: "…my mastery and professionalism."	(Page 4)
	Cross-fade to spot UC	
Cue 10	**Hannah**: "But she is reputed to be the best."	(Page 4)
	Change to full general lighting	
Cue 11	**Hannah** helps **Dawn** to her "room"	(Page 16)
	Cross-fade to spot UL	
Cue 12	**Dawn**: "But Jones scares me."	(Page 16)
	Cross-fade to spot UR	
Cue 13	**Jones**: "I'm nothing … we're all nothing."	(Page 16)
	Change to full general lighting	
Cue 14	**Jones** slumps into the chair behind the table	(Page 30)
	Cross-fade to pool of light spilling over table	

EFFECTS PLOT

Cue 1   To open   (Page 1)
               Play Windmills of Your Mind, *increasing on*
                  Curtain rise

Cue 2   Spots light up   (Page 1)
               Fade music

Cue 3   To close   (Page 31)
               Play Windmills of Your Mind